Library of Congress Cataloging-in-Publication Data

Spencer, Diana L., 1960-
    Abraham Lincoln / written by Diana L. Spencer ;
illustrated by Isidre Mones.
        p.   cm. — (Great leaders)
    Summary: Simple text and illustrations depict the life and
achievements of Abraham Lincoln.
    ISBN 0-517-06996-2 (hardcover) :
    1. Lincoln, Abraham, 1809-1865—Juvenile literature.
2. Presidents—United States—Biography—Juvenile literature.
[1. Lincoln, Abraham, 1809-1865.   2. Presidents.]   I. Mones,
Isidre, ill. II. Title. III. Series.
E457.905.S66   1991
973.7'092—dc20
    [B]   91-33928
                                                                                                CIP
                                                                                                 AC

Abraham Lincoln

Written by Diana L. Spencer

Illustrated by Isidre Mones

DERRYDALE BOOKS
New York

Government of the people, by the people, for the people, shall not perish from this earth.

Abraham Lincoln
Gettysburg Address

Meet
Abe Lincoln

A small one-room log cabin in Kentucky with one tiny window and a dirt floor does not sound like a special place, but it was. It was where Abraham Lincoln, the sixteenth president of the United States, was born on February 12, 1809.

Lincoln is one of the most respected United States' presidents. While he was president, several states tried to form their own separate country. Lincoln brought the country back together.

The United States was still a small country when Abe was growing up. There were only about twenty-five states. Much of the country, including Kentucky, was still wilderness.

Growing up in the wilderness was not easy for Abe or his older sister, Sarah. There was little time for play. The family had to grow their own food and make most of their own tools. Abe helped his father with many chores. He helped plant and harvest crops, pull weeds, and chop firewood.

At night, Abe was very tired. But he was never too tired to stretch out in front of the fireplace and read. One of his favorite books was about George Washington. He thought Washington was a great man.

Abe wanted to go to school, but his father thought it was a waste of time. He needed Abe's help on the farm. Abe's mother insisted that her children go to school in the winter, when the farm work was slow.

Abe and Sarah walked several miles to a one-room schoolhouse. The school was called a "blab" school because the students said their lessons out loud. Some students said, "Two plus two is four." Others said, "C-A-T spells cat." Abe's voice always could be heard above the others.

When Abe was seven, his family moved to Indiana. He continued to read whenever he could, even when he was plowing. For two years, the family worked hard on their farm. Then, disaster struck. Abe's mother got sick and died. Abe was sad.

After a year, Abe's father decided to take a trip to Kentucky. Many months later he returned married to Sarah Bush Johnston.

Abe grew to love his stepmother very much. One reason was that she sent him to school more often. Abe learned to write poetry. One day, he wrote:

> Abraham Lincoln
> his hand and pen,
> he will be good
> but God knows when.

Abe Sees More of the World

When Abe was eighteen, his sister Sarah died. Once again, he was sad.

Shortly after Sarah's death, a farmer hired Abe to build a flatboat and take hogs and corn to the market in New Orleans. The farmer's son, Allen, went with Abe. This was Abe's first trip without his family. He was very excited and just a little bit scared. Once he started sailing, though, he was fine.

The trip down the Ohio and Mississippi Rivers took many days. At night, Abe and Allen tied the boat to shore and slept until morning. One night, a group of men tried to steal the boat. Abe and Allen fought off the men. Afterwards, they were afraid to stay near land. They sailed the rest of the way without stopping.

New Orleans was a new and exciting world to Abe. He had never seen a city. But one thing shocked and upset him. Slavery. He saw black men, women, and children chained together and sold like animals. Southern plantation owners used the slaves to plant and harvest tobacco and cotton. Slavery was not common in the North or on the western frontier.

Abe was happy to go home.

Leaving Home

When Abe turned twenty-one, he decided it was time to leave home and be on his own. He moved to New Salem, Illinois, and got a job working in a store.

One day, a woman came to the store and forgot to take home half of the tea she had bought. Abe walked many miles to bring her the tea. Because Abe was so honest and thoughtful, people started calling him ''Honest Abe.''

After a while, Abe and his friend, William Berry, decided to open their own store. At first many people came. But soon that changed. When Berry was in charge of the store, he often closed it and left. The store did not make money. Abe and his friend were forced to close it.

Abe worried because he owed many people money. He had to pay them back. He started doing odd jobs to earn extra money. President Andrew Jackson paid Abe forty-eight cents a week to deliver mail once a week. But Abe still needed more money. He worked on farms and at the local gristmill. He taught himself to

be a surveyor, someone who measures land and makes maps of it. He also studied to be a lawyer.

The townspeople were proud that Abe worked so hard to pay back the money he owed. They liked him more than ever. You are honest, they told him, you should go into government and help make laws for the state.

Abe was worried. He had run in an election once before and lost. That wouldn't happen again, he decided. He traveled all over the state telling people why they should vote for him. He said he would try to get better roads built in their towns. He promised to vote for free public schools where all children could learn to read and write.

While the votes were being counted, Abe was very nervous. He didn't want to lose. This time, Abe won! He became an Illinois state legislator.

Soon, a happy Abe left for his new job at the state capitol. He was very busy. People who walked into his office laughed at the tall stacks of paper on his desk. When Abe left the office, he carried the papers he needed in his stovepipe hat. For eight years, Abe worked in the state government. People listened to his ideas and they trusted him.

Even though he worked hard, Abe still found time to have fun. One night, at a party, Abe met Mary Todd. Mary was smart, pleasant, and pretty. For a while, Abe just stared at her. Then he walked over to her and said, "Miss Todd, I should like to dance with you in the worst way."

After they danced, Mary laughed and said, "Mr. Lincoln danced just the way he said he would. He danced in the worst way." Abe liked Mary's sense of humor.

Mary and Abe fell in love. On November 4, 1842, they were married. At first, they could only afford to rent a room above a tavern. Soon though, they bought a nice house. Within a few years, they had two sons, Robert and Edward.

Abe always found time to play with his sons. Sometimes he took them to his messy office and let them play while he worked. Often, he carried them around on his shoulders.

Mary tried to teach Abe better manners. She asked him to sit on a chair instead of the floor. She tried to get him to wear shoes in the house instead of walking barefoot. But Abe didn't change his ways. He wanted to be comfortable in his own home.

On to Washington

all men are created equal

The Great Debates

By 1854, the Lincolns had two more sons, William and Thomas. Their son Edward had died.

For a while, Abraham Lincoln worked in Washington, D.C., as a congressman making laws for the country.

After Lincoln left Washington, many Southerners started asking Congress to allow slavery in the western territories. Northerners did not like this idea.

Senator Stephen Douglas sided with the Southerners. Douglas proposed the Kansas-Nebraska law. This law said the people in these territories could decide for themselves if they wanted to own slaves.

Lincoln was upset by this law. He believed slavery was wrong and did not want it to spread. Lincoln reminded people that the Constitution said all men are created equal. He decided to run against Douglas in the next election.

Lincoln proposed a series of seven debates, which came to be known as The Great Debates. In front of an audience, he met with Douglas and they argued for and against the new law.

Lincoln lost the election, but many people heard about what he

had said in the debates. He was now famous for his ideas, sense of justice, and intelligence.

Lincoln for President

In 1860, Lincoln and Douglas both ran for President of the United States. This time Lincoln won! It should have been a happy time, but Lincoln was sad. He said to a group of reporters, "Well, boys, your troubles are now over, mine have just begun."

He was sad because many Southerners were afraid that he would outlaw slavery. Slavery was the only way they could survive, Southerners argued. By this time, there were 3 million slaves in the South.

Seven southern states decided to start their own country, the Confederate States of America. They made their own flag and elected Jefferson Davis their president. In their country, slavery could not be stopped.

Lincoln was heartbroken. He felt troubled that the United States was breaking apart because of him. More than anything he wanted the United States together. He was afraid that other states might leave. He wasn't sure what to do.

The Civil War

On Lincoln's first day as president, he said that the United States could not be a "house divided." He claimed the Confederate States were still part of the United States and asked them to come back. "We are not enemies, but friends," he said. "We must not be enemies." Lincoln also promised not to fight the Confederates unless they attacked the United States.

Lincoln had another problem. Fort Sumter, which belonged to the United States, was in South Carolina, a Confederate state. The men in the fort were running out of supplies. Lincoln decided to send supplies and reinforcements, but before help arrived the Confederate Army attacked Fort Sumter.

The Civil War had started. Lincoln asked men to join his army. Four more states joined the Confederate side. The states still left in the United States were called the Union states.

The North had more men and more guns. People in the North thought the war would be over quickly. They soon learned otherwise. The Confederate states had great generals. They also had many people who wanted to win.

A long, bloody war had started.

Lincoln hated war. He hated to see so many young men dying. It was especially hard to see people who had been neighbors and friends now fighting against each other.

As much as he hated war, Lincoln was proud of the Union states. He was proud of the young men who were fighting. When he saw them on the street, he took off his hat and bowed. Sometimes, he went to the hospitals and visited soldiers who were sick and hurt.

In the middle of the war, the President's son, William, became ill and died. Now, more than ever, the President knew how the families of the soldiers felt. He was so sad that he couldn't eat. He lost twenty-five pounds. Sometimes Lincoln would say, ''I shall never live to see peace. This war is killing me.''

As the war continued, more and more people wanted to end slavery. Mary Lincoln was one of them. She had become good friends with a White House dressmaker named Elizabeth Keckley. Elizabeth had been a slave. She told Mary how slaves were beaten and sold. After hearing Elizabeth's stories, Mary begged Abe to do something.

On January 1, 1863, President Abraham Lincoln issued the Emancipation Proclamation, which stated that the Confederate slaves were now free. It asked black men to fight in the war on the Union side. Thousands of slaves ran away from the South and went to help the North win the war.

On November 19, 1863, President Lincoln went to Gettysburg, Pennsylvania. Seven thousand soldiers had died in a battle there. Now, 15,000 people had come to remember them.

When Lincoln spoke, he said that the soldiers had died so the United States of America could live. He said, ''This nation, under God, shall have a new birth of freedom—and that government of the people, by the people, for the people, shall not perish from the earth.''

His speech was called the Gettysburg Address. It was only ten sentences long, but it is still famous today.

In 1864, while the war went on, Lincoln was elected president again. A big party was held. Outside, Lincoln heard people yelling. The guards were trying to stop a black writer named

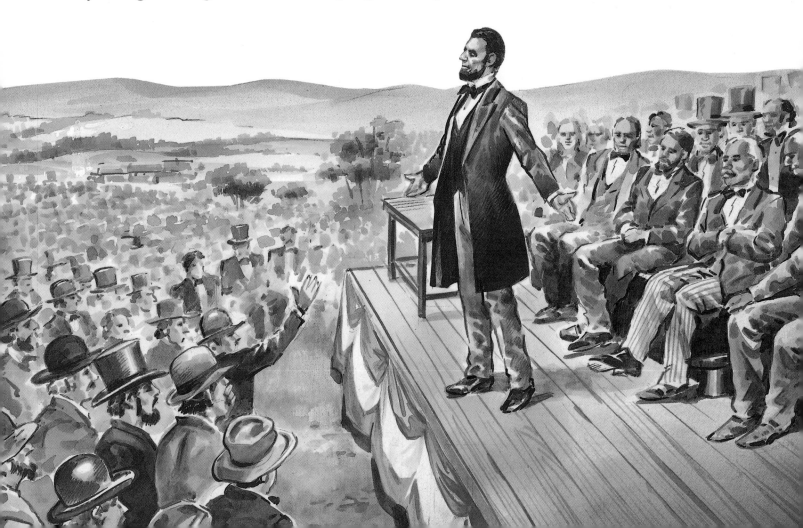

Frederick Douglass from going in. Douglass wanted to thank Lincoln for stopping slavery. No black person had ever attended a White House party before. But Lincoln told the guards to let Douglass come in.

The next year, the United States Congress outlawed slavery in all the states.

On April 9, 1865, as flowers bloomed around Washington, D.C., General Robert E. Lee, of the Confederate Army, surrendered to General Ulysses S. Grant, of the Union Army, at Appomattox Courthouse in Virginia. The North had won. Once again, the United States was one country.

Lincoln started looking ahead. Most of the war had been fought in the South. It had lasted more than four years. More than 618,000 soldiers had died. Many homes and businesses were destroyed. President Lincoln knew he had to help people in the South rebuild. He knew he had to help the freed slaves find jobs and places to live. There was much work ahead.

A Man We Won't Forget

Even with all the work he had to do, Abraham Lincoln was happy again. The United States was one country and the terrible war was over. On April 14, 1865, Abe and Mary Lincoln decided to go to a play at Ford's Theater in Washington, D.C.

As they sat there laughing, a man named John Wilkes Booth sneaked up behind Abraham Lincoln. Before anyone could stop Booth, he shot Lincoln in the back of the head and ran away.

Lincoln died the next morning. He was only fifty-six years old. He was the first president to be assassinated.

Booth was caught, but he died in a barn fire before he could be brought to trial.

A train carried Lincoln's body back to Springfield, Illinois, to be buried. As the train passed through towns, people stood by the tracks crying and waving goodbye.

Abraham Lincoln was a great president. He reunited the country and freed the slaves.

People still remember Lincoln today. Each year many people visit the Lincoln Memorial, a nineteen-foot statue in Washington, D.C., to pay him tribute.

Important Dates

1809   Abraham Lincoln born in Kentucky
1816   Family moves to Indiana
1818   Mother dies
1819   Father marries Sarah Bush Johnston
1828   Sister Sarah dies
1830   Moves with family to Illinois
1834   Elected to Illinois state legislature
1837   Moves to Springfield
1842   Marries Mary Todd
1843   Son Robert born
1846   Son Edward born
       Elected to United States Congress
1850   Son Edward dies
       Son William born
1853   Son Thomas born
1858   Great Debates
       Loses election to Stephen A. Douglas
1860   Elected sixteenth president of the United States
1861   Civil War begins
1862   Son William dies
1863   Writes and signs Emancipation Proclamation
       Gives Gettysburg Address
1864   Reelected president
1865   Civil War ends
       Lincoln shot and killed